Greece
Profile of Health and Well-being

Abstract

Profiles of health and well-being give an overview of a country's health status, describing data on mortality, morbidity and exposure to key risk factors together with trends over time. They are developed in collaboration with WHO European Member States. When possible, each report also compares a country to a reference group, which is in this report the whole WHO European Region and the European Union member countries prior to 1 May 2004. To make the comparisons as valid as possible, data are as a rule taken from one source to ensure that they have been harmonized in a reasonably consistent way. The data in the report are drawn from the European Health for All (HFA) database of the WHO Regional Office for Europe. The HFA data are collected from Member States on an annual basis and include metadata that specify the original source of data for specific indicators.

Keywords

HEALTH STATUS, COST OF ILLNESS, LIFE EXPECTANCY, COMPARATIVE STUDY, HEALTH SYSTEMS PLANS, DELIVERY OF HEALTH CARE, GREECE

Address requests about publications of the WHO Regional Office for Europe to:

Publications
WHO Regional Office for Europe
UN City, Marmorvej 51
DK-2100 Copenhagen Ø
Denmark

Alternatively, complete an online request form for documentation, health information, or for permission to quote or translate, on the Regional Office website (http://www.euro.who.int/pubrequest).

ISBN 978 92 890 5143 9

Design: ref-point.net.

Greece
Profile of Health and Well-being

World Health Organization
REGIONAL OFFICE FOR Europe

Contents

Acknowledgements

The highlights on health and well-being and accompanying profiles of health and well-being are produced under the overall direction of Claudia Stein, Director, Division of Information, Evidence, Research and Innovation, WHO Regional Office for Europe.

The principal authors of this publication were:

- Mika Gissler, Consultant, WHO Regional Office for Europe, and Research Professor, National Institute for Health and Welfare, Finland;
- Ivo Rakovac, Programme Manager a.i., Health Information, Monitoring and Analysis, WHO Regional Office for Europe;
- Nadia Scott, Consultant, WHO Regional Office for Europe;
- Claudia Stein, Director, Division of Information, Evidence, Research and Innovation, WHO Regional Office for Europe.

Other contributors included Charalampos Economou, Panteion University of Social and Political Sciences, Athens, Greece, and João Breda, Silviu Domente, and Sarah Thomson, WHO Regional Office for Europe.

Abbreviations and acronyms

EU European Union

EU15 countries belonging to the EU before 1 May 2004

GDP gross domestic product

HFA Health for All (database)

ICD International Classification of Diseases

PPP purchasing power parity

Summary of situation and trends in health and well-being in Greece

Historically, the health status of the Greek population was among the best in the WHO European Region. The improvement in health status, as measured by life expectancy and mortality, has continued, but more slowly than the average for the countries belonging to the European Union before 1 May 2004 (EU15). The most recent life expectancy at birth for males (79 years) equals the EU15 average, while women are expected to live one year less (83 years) than their counterparts in the EU15. Healthy life expectancy increased to 69 years for men and to 73 years for women by 2013.

The slow rise in life expectancy is mainly a function of the slow improvement in mortality from diseases of the circulatory system and malignant neoplasms (cancers) in comparison with the EU15. The mortality rate from diseases of the respiratory system has in fact increased, reflecting the high proportion of regular daily smokers. The already low mortality rates from infectious diseases and external causes of injuries and poisoning have continued to fall, apart from mortality from motor vehicle traffic accidents for which Greece has the highest rate in the EU. Premature mortality, particularly from cardiovascular diseases, is substantially higher in Greece than the EU15 average.

The incidence of infectious disease is in general low, excluding the rates for HIV and AIDS, which have rapidly increased during the last few years. Vaccination coverage is high.

The health system is curative-oriented. No referral system has been established and the network of public health services is underdeveloped. It is also characterized by a high density of physicians, low density of nurses and high hospitalization rates. Total health expenditure is in line with the EU15 average, but the share of out-of-pocket expenditure is very high.

Since 2009, the Greek economic crisis has negatively affected the health status of the population. Notably, the numbers of infant and maternal deaths have increased, as have suicides and homicides (for males only).

Monitoring of the Health 2020 targets[1] (see table below) has shown improved trends for 10 out of 19 core indicators. Deteriorating trends have been noted for three indicators: the prevalence of overweight, the unemployment rate and the Gini coefficient on income distribution. Greece is on track to reach the regional target for the reduction of premature mortality from four major noncommunicable diseases (cardiovascular diseases, cancer, diabetes mellitus and chronic respiratory diseases) but not for diseases of the digestive system.

Core indicators for monitoring Health 2020 policy targets in Greece, most recent years available

Target	Indicator	Value			Year
		Male	Female	Total	
1. Reduce premature mortality[a]	Premature mortality rate from cardiovascular disease, cancer, diabetes mellitus and chronic respiratory diseases among people aged 30 to under 70 years	365	161	259	2011
	Prevalence of tobacco use among adults aged 18 years and over[b] *(5)*	51.2	25.7	38.2	2013
	Pure alcohol consumption per capita among adults aged 15 years and over	–	–	7.4	2011
	Prevalence of overweight and obese (body mass index ≥25) adults aged 18 years and over (age-standardized estimate) *(6)*	66	55	61	2014
	Mortality rate from external causes of injury and poisoning, all ages	42	11	26	2011
2. Increase life expectancy	Life expectancy at birth, in years	78.6	83.2	80.9	2011
3. Reduce inequities[c]	Infant mortality rate per 1000 live births	3.2	2.6	2.9	2012
	Proportion of children of official primary school age not enrolled (net enrolment rate *(7)*)	0.8	0.2	0.5	2011
	Unemployment *(8)*	23.6	30.2	26.5	2014
	National policy addressing reduction of health inequities established and documented	NA	NA	No	NA
	Gini coefficient *(9)*	–	–	0.37	2012
4. Enhance well-being[d]	Life satisfaction among adults aged 15 years and older *(10)*	–	–	5.1	2007–2012
	Availability of social support among adults aged 50 years and older *(10)*	–	–	61	2013
	Percentage of population with improved sanitation facilities *(11)*	–	–	99	2015
5. Universal coverage and "right to health"	Private household out-of-pocket expenditure as proportion of total health expenditure	NA	NA	26.4	2013
	Percentage of children vaccinated against measles (one dose by second birthday)	–	–	99	2012
	Percentage of children vaccinated against poliomyelitis (three doses by first birthday)	–	–	99	2012
	Percentage of children vaccinated against rubella (one dose by second birthday)	–	–	99	2012
	Total health expenditure as a percentage of gross domestic product	NA	NA	9.8	2013
6. National targets	Establishment of process for target-setting documented	NA	NA	No	2015
	Evidence documenting:				
	(a) national health service aligned with Health 2020	NA	NA	No	2015
	(b) implementation plan	NA	NA	No	2015
	(c) accountability mechanism	NA	NA	No	2015

NA: not applicable.
[a] Target 1 includes percentage of children vaccinated against measles, poliomyelitis and rubella.
[b] Prevalence includes both daily and occasional (less than daily) use among adults aged 15 years or more.
[c] Target 3 includes life expectancy at birth.
[d] Target 4 includes Gini coefficient, the unemployment rate and the proportion of children not enrolled in primary school.
Source: WHO European Health for All database *(9)* unless otherwise specified.

[1] WHO's policy framework supporting action across government and society for health and well-being.

Life satisfaction (a measure of subjective well-being) is lower in Greece than the average for the Region and the EU15. Among objective well-being measures, 61% of people aged over 50 years reported that they had relatives or friends on whom they could count when in trouble, which is among the lowest proportion in the Region. A national health policy aligned with Health 2020, including an implementation plan and accountability mechanism, has been developed but not yet formally adopted.

References

1. Global Adult Tobacco Survey: Greece 2013. Copenhagen: WHO Regional Office for Europe; 2015 (http://www.who.int/tobacco/surveillance/survey/gats/grc/en/, accessed 13 December 2015).
2. Global Health Observatory (GHO) data [online database]. Geneva: World Health Organization; 2015 (http://www.who.int/gho/en/, accessed 12 March 2016).
3. UIS.STAT [online database]. Montreal: UNESCO Institute for Statistics; 2016 (http://www.uis.unesco.org/Pages/default.aspx, accessed 12 March 2016).
4. ILOSTAT database [online database]. Geneva: International Labour Organization; 2016 (http://www.ilo.org/ilostat/faces/help_home/data_by_country/country-details?_adf.ctrl-state=3wmg83w82_25&_afrLoop=552577240791405, accessed 12 March 2016).
5. GINI index (World Bank estimate) [online database]. Washington (DC): World Bank; 2016 (http://data.worldbank.org/indicator/SI.POV.GINI, accessed 12 March 2016).
6. UNDP human development reports. Human Development Index (HDI) [website]. New York (NY): United Nations Development Programme; 2016 (http://hdr.undp.org/en/content/human-development-index-hdi, accessed 12 March 2016).
7. Targets and indicators for Health 2020: Version 2. Copenhagen: WHO Regional Office for Europe; 2014 (http://www.euro.who.int/__data/assets/pdf_file/0009/251775/Health-2020-Targets-and-indicators-version2-ENG.pdf?ua=1, accessed 15 December 2015).
8. WHO/UNICEF Joint Monitoring Programme (JMP) for Water Supply and Sanitation [online database]. Geneva: World Health Organization; 2015 (http://www.wssinfo.org/, accessed 15 December 2015).
9. European Health for All database (HFA-DB) [online database]. Copenhagen: WHO Regional Office for Europe; 2015 (http://data.euro.who.int/hfadb/, accessed 15 December 2015).

Introduction

In 2012, WHO European Member States adopted Health 2020 *(1,2)*, a policy framework supporting action across government and society for health and well-being. With the accelerated implementation of Health 2020, the WHO Regional Office for Europe has introduced two new series, the profiles of health and well-being and the highlights on health and well-being. These follow on from the highlights on health series, which ran from the early 1990s to the mid-2000s with the aim of addressing the need for analyses of the health situation and trends in newly emerging states in order to assist European countries with evidence-informed policy-making. The profiles of health and well-being provide comparative analyses of the situation and trends in health and well-being in countries, describing recent data on mortality, morbidity and exposure to key risk factors and giving special emphasis to all Health 2020 indicators *(3)*, including well-being. They are developed in collaboration with Member States and do not constitute a formal statistical publication. The highlights on health and well-being form a separate series, with policy-makers as the target audience, highlighting the main findings from the longer Profiles.

To make the comparisons as valid as possible, data are taken from a single source to ensure that they are harmonized consistently. Unless otherwise noted, data in the reports are drawn from the European Health for All (HFA) database[1] of the Regional Office *(4)*. The HFA data are collected from Member States and other international sources on an annual basis and include metadata that specify the original source of data for specific indicators. Other data and information used in the report are referenced accordingly. The International Classification of Diseases, tenth edition (ICD-10) codes for causes of death are given in Annex 1. When possible, each report also compares a country to one or more reference groups of countries, which in this report are all the WHO European Member States and the countries belonging to the European Union before May 2004 (EU15), including Greece.

[1] The HFA database *(4)* covers data since 1970. The reference year is 2000.

Selected demographic and economic information

The WHO European Region as a whole is faced with a below-replacement birth rate and a rapidly ageing population. These trends are particularly heightened in Greece and may impose additional economic pressure in the coming years. Since 2009, the total fertility rate in Greece (1.34 in 2012) has fallen 18% below that of the Region and is nearing lowest-low levels, substantially below the theoretical replacement level of 2.1 (Fig. 1). This decline, combined with increased longevity, has transformed the population structure (Fig. 2). In 2011, the group aged 0–14 years comprised just 14.4% of the total population, compared to 15.8% for the EU15 and 16.9% for the Region (Fig. 3, Table 1). At the other end of the spectrum, those over the age of 65 years now form 19.5% of the total population, representing an increase of almost three percentage points since 2000 (Table 1, Fig. 4). Given these trends, it is not surprising that natural population growth is again negative, falling below 2000 levels (Table 1). Low growth and high levels of emigration have contributed to a decrease in the total population, such that the 2014 population level was the lowest observed since 2000 *(5)*.

Greece's real gross domestic product (GDP, expressed in dollar purchasing power parity (PPP) per capita) fell sharply following

Fig. 1. **Total fertility rate,** Greece, WHO European Region and EU15, 1980–2012

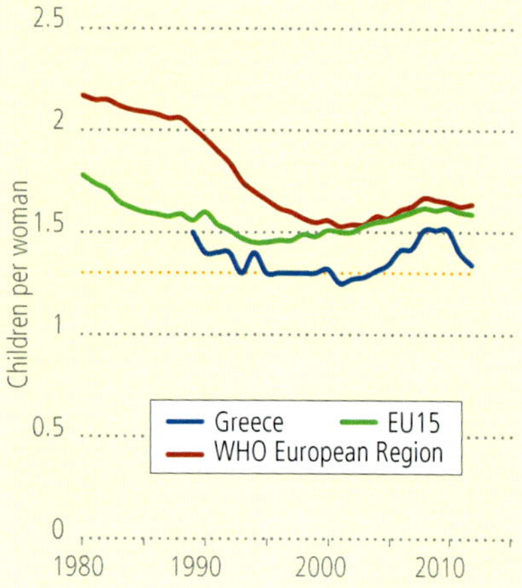

Fig. 2. **Population structure by age and sex,** Greece, 1980 and 2011

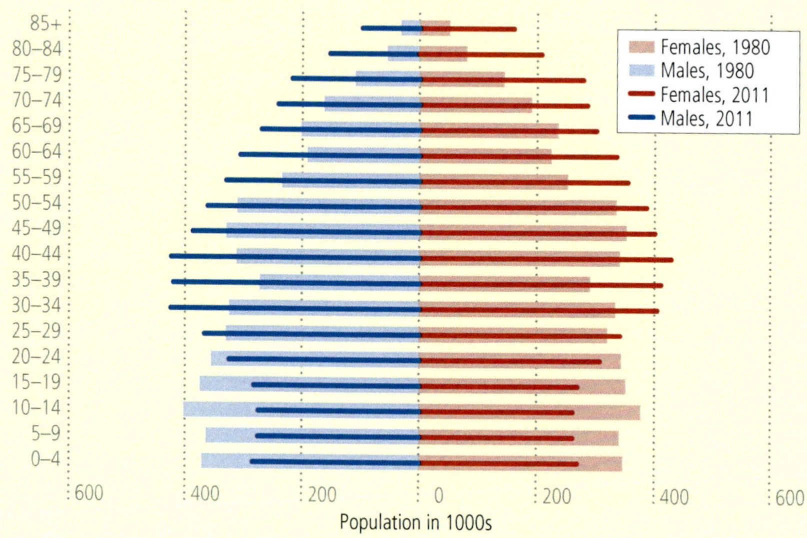

the economic crisis that began in 2009. It has, however, remained consistently above 2000 levels, while not recovering to the extent of the Region as a whole and the EU15. Although the unemployment rate remains the highest in the EU at 26.5% *(6)*, positive improvements are evident with regard to reducing inequalities between the sexes. Although women are more likely to be unemployed than men, in both the short and long terms, the gap between the sexes has narrowed since 2000 *(6)*. Of the total unemployed population, however, 74% have been unemployed for over 12 months, representing an increase of 17 percentage points over 2000 levels *(6)* and signifying a potential health burden for the unemployed and their dependants.

Fig. 3. **Percentage of population aged 0–14 years,** Greece, WHO European Region and EU15, 1980–2011

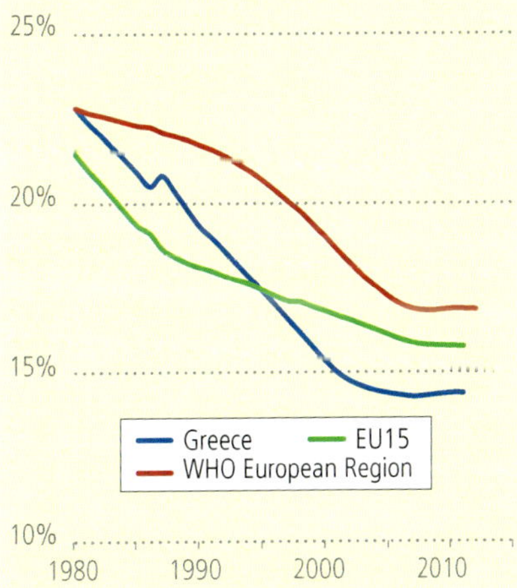

Fig. 4. **Percentage of population aged 65+ years,** Greece, WHO European Region and EU15, 1980–2011

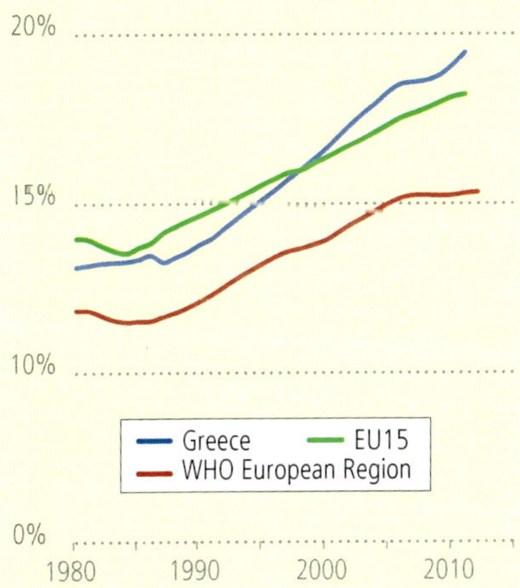

Table 1. **Selected demographic indicators,** Greece, WHO European Region and EU15, 2012 or latest available year

Indicators	Greece	WHO European Region	EU15
Population (in 000s)	11 093	902 367	398 635
Percentage aged 0–14 years	14.4	16.8	15.8
Percentage aged 15–64 years	66.2	67.8	66
Percentage aged 65 years or more	19.5	15.3	18.2
Percentage urban	61.4	70.3	76.8
Crude birth rate (live births per 1000)	9.4	12	10.5
Crude death rate per 1000	9.8	10.5	9.3
Natural population growth per 1000[a]	-0.4	1.5	1.2

[a] Birth rate minus death rate.

Source: WHO *(4)*.

Health status and burden of disease

Life expectancy

Life expectancy at birth is defined as the average number of years that a newborn infant would live if prevailing patterns of mortality at the time of birth were to continue throughout his or her life. Historically, Greece has had one of the highest, steadily increasing rates of life expectancy in Europe. The increase in life expectancy has, however, been outstripped by that in the EU15, such that the life expectancy for both females and males in 2011 was less than that of their counterparts in the EU15 (Fig. 5, 6). In 2011, life expectancy in Greece (78.6 years for men and 83.2 years for women) was still substantially higher than the average for the Region (73.1 years and 80.3 years, respectively).

Life expectancy at 65 years, defined as the average number of years a 65-year-old would expect to live based on prevailing mortality statistics, has followed the same trends as life expectancy at birth (Fig. 7, 8). Life expectancy for males rose at the same rate as the EU15 average after 2000 to a high of 18.6 years in 2011. In the same time period, life expectancy for females was on average 1.5 years less than for females overall in the EU15.

Fig. 5. **Life expectancy at birth for males,** Greece, WHO European Region and EU15, 1980–2011

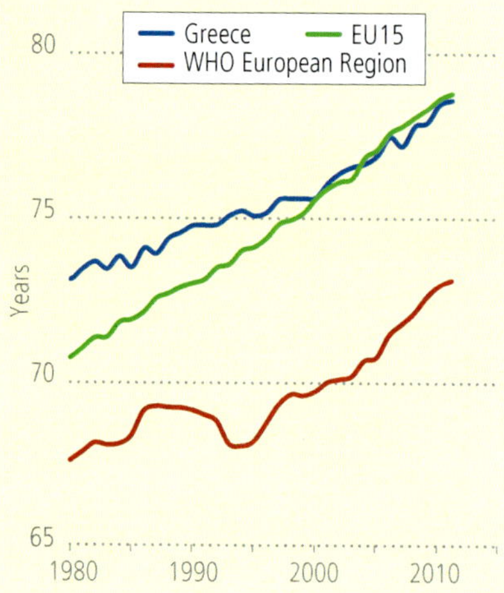

Fig. 6. **Life expectancy at birth for females,** Greece, WHO European Region and EU15, 1980–2011

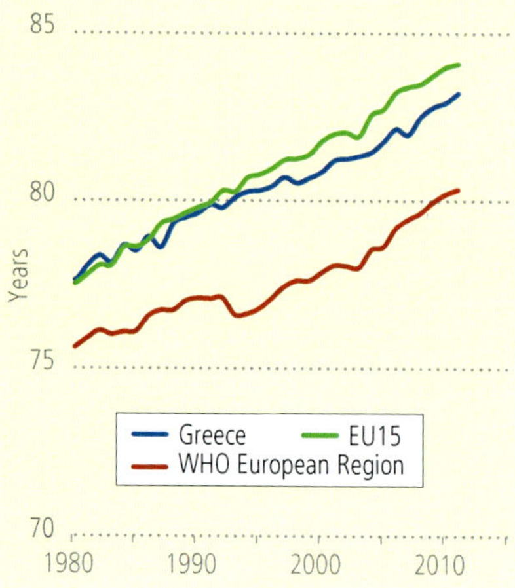

Fig. 7. **Life expectancy at 65 years for males,** Greece, WHO European Region and EU15, 1980–2011

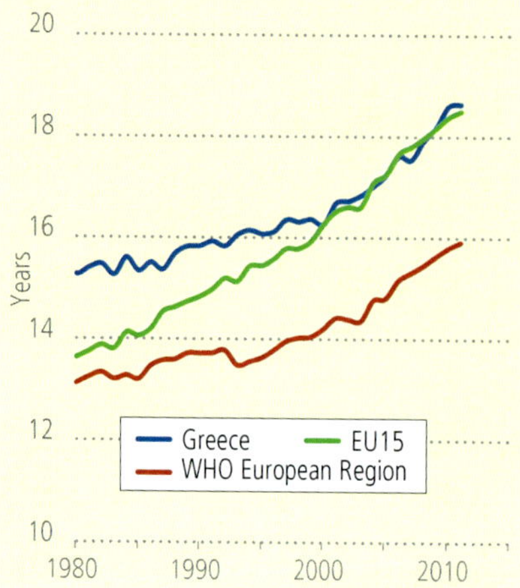

Fig. 8. **Life expectancy at 65 years for females,** Greece, WHO European Region and EU15, 1980–2011

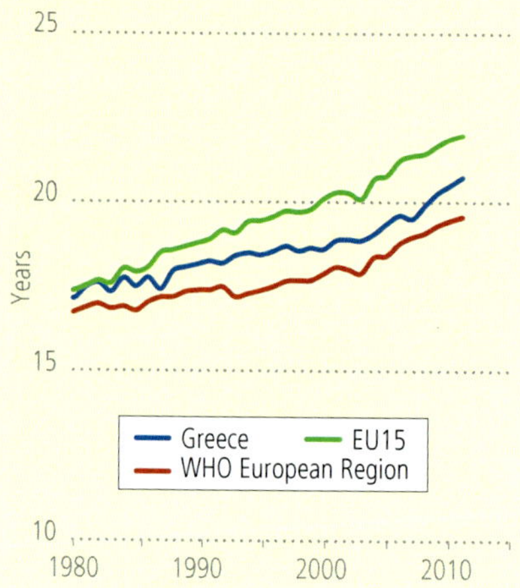

Healthy life expectancy and disability-adjusted life-years

Healthy life expectancy summarizes mortality and non-fatal outcomes in a single measure of average population health. It has been used to compare health between countries and to measure changes over time.

Data for Greece *(7)* show that healthy life expectancy increased by two years to 69 years for men and by four years to 73 years for women between 2000 and 2013. These estimates were half a year higher than the EU15 averages but three to five years higher than the estimates for the Region (64 years for men and 70 years for women in 2013).

Fig. 9. **Tuberculosis incidence per 100 000 population,** Greece, WHO European Region and EU15, 1980–2012

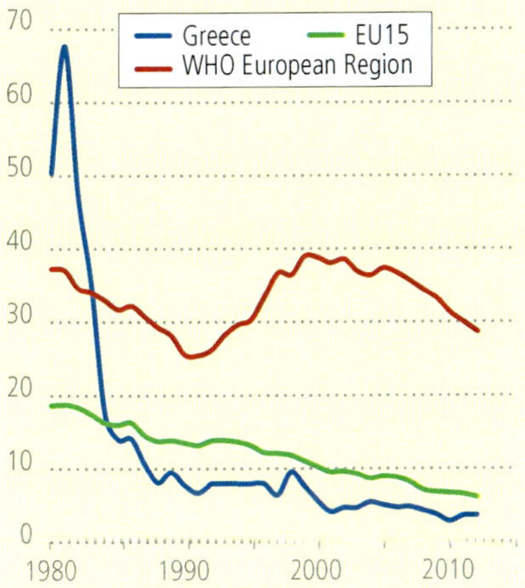

Morbidity

Comparable information on morbidity is more limited than for mortality. Data are, however, available on certain infectious diseases, cancers and mental disorders based on routine health reporting systems. The coverage, completeness and quality of these data vary between countries and over time and comparisons should be interpreted with caution. Primary sources of data are diverse and include registries, surveillance systems and hospitals.

Infectious diseases and vaccinations

The reported incidences of tuberculosis (Fig. 9), hepatitis A, hepatitis B, pertussis, measles, diphtheria, poliomyelitis, rubella and mumps in Greece are below the averages of the EU15 and the Region. There are no recent data on the incidences of syphilis or gonorrhoea.

Fig. 10. **HIV incidence per 100 000 population,** Greece, WHO European Region and EU15, 1980–2012

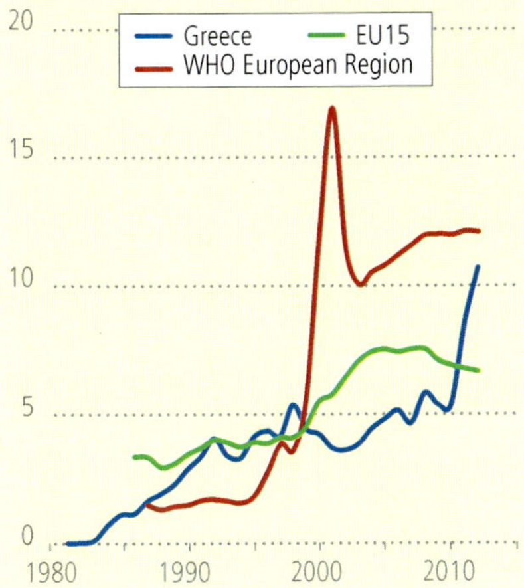

The incidence of HIV has increased substantially (Fig. 10). It remained at or under 5/100 000 from 2000 until 2011–2012, when it increased rapidly in contrast to the EU15 average, which showed a slight decline. In 2012, the incidence in Greece (10.7/100 000) was 60% higher than the EU15 average (6.7/100 000) although below the average for the Region (12.1/100 000). The incidence of AIDS has been consistently low: between 2001 and 2012 it was below 1/100 000. As with the HIV incidence rate, the AIDS rate in 2012 (0.97/100 000) was above the average for the EU15 (0.88/100 000) but below the average for the Region (1.27/100 000).

Overall, trends in vaccination rates for diphtheria, tetanus, pertussis, measles, rubella and poliomyelitis are high and above regional and EU15 averages (99%) (Fig. 11a and b). The vaccination rate for hepatitis B has remained high at 95%, and the rate for

Haemophilius influenzae type b increased from below 90% in 2000–2011 to 94% in 2012.

Other diseases

The availability of information for other diseases in the HFA database is very limited. There is no recent information on the incidence and prevalence of cancer and mental disorders from Greece. The Greek incidence of alcohol psychosis was 20/100 000 in 2008, or one fifth of the average for the Region (97/100 000).

Fig. 11a. **Percentage of children with measles immunization,** Greece, WHO European Region and EU15, 1980–2012

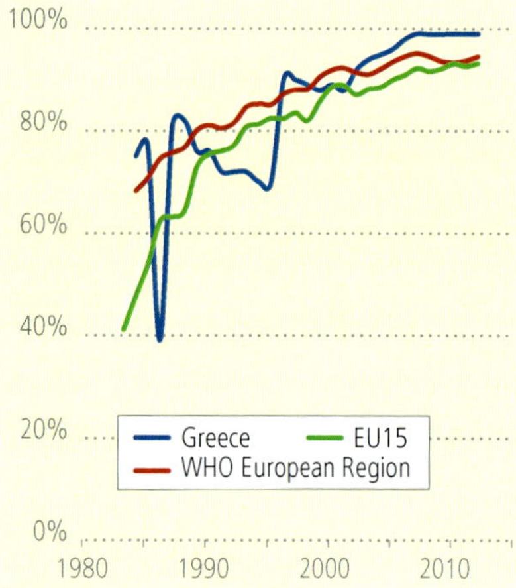

Infant and maternal mortality

The infant mortality rate per 1000 live births in Greece declined for decades and was below the EU15 average in 2003–2009 (Fig. 12). In 2009–2011 it was, however, almost one third higher (3.4 per 1000 live births) than in 2008 (2.7/1000). At the same time, the EU15 average decreased by 2%.

The maternal mortality ratio has been very low, below the EU15 average for decades in Greece (Fig. 13). The latest available three-year rolling average for 2009–2011 showed, however, an increase to 4.1 per 100 000 live births. Even so, this is still lower than the EU15 average of 5.3 per 100 000 and the regional average of 13.1 per 100 000.

Fig. 11b. **Percentage of infants with poliomyelitis immunization,** Greece, WHO European Region and EU15, 1980–2012

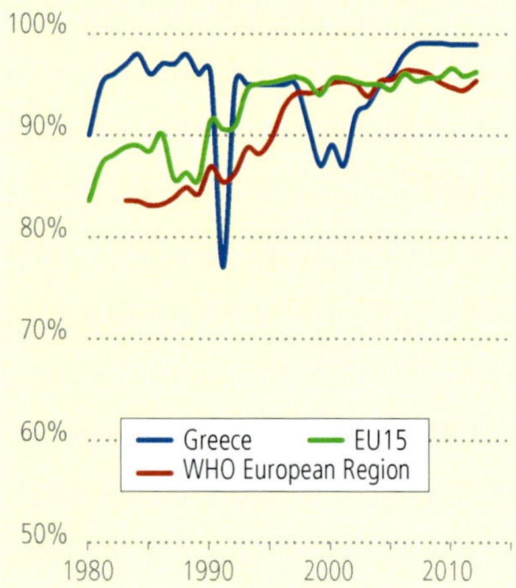

Leading causes of death

A comparison of age-standardized mortality rates[2] between countries highlights population differences in the most common causes of death, allowing an easier identification of which deaths could be prevented. Cause of death data are classified using the ICD *(8)*, a complex statistical classification. As considerable differences in certification and coding practices exist between countries, the results should be viewed with caution. Greece is one of the only two countries in the Region still using the ninth revision of the ICD, which further limits the comparability of cause of death data.

Age-standardized mortality from all causes is higher in Greece than the average for the EU15, and is explained by excess mortality from

[2] Age-standardized death rates are calculated using the direct method: that is, they represent what the crude rates would have been were the population to have had the same age distribution as the standard European population.

diseases of the circulatory system and of the respiratory system. Deaths from diseases of the circulatory system, malignant neoplasms (cancers) and external causes of injury and poisoning (accidents, homicides and suicides) are the main killers in the Region, causing 75% of all deaths. In Greece, the share was slightly lower at 72% in 2011, even though the EU15 average was even lower, at 67%.

Fig. 12. **Infant deaths per 1000 live births,** Greece, WHO European Region and EU15, 1980–2012

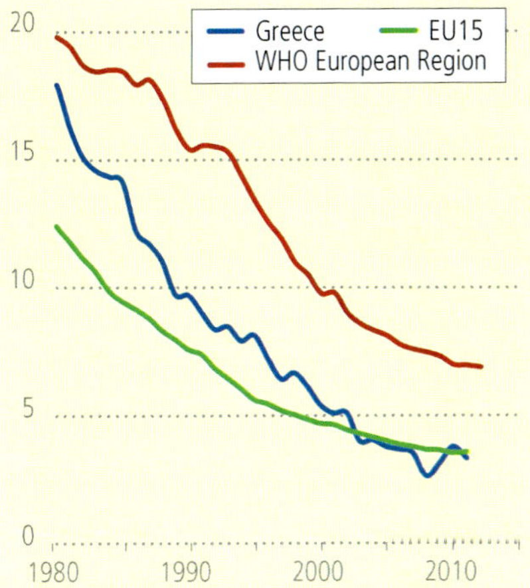

The Greek figure for premature mortality (before the age of 65 years) is at the same level as the EU15 average, even though mortality from diseases of the circulatory system and of the respiratory system and external causes of injury and poisoning is higher in Greece than the average for the EU15 (Fig. 14).

The trends in age-standardized death rates for diseases of the circulatory system, malignant neoplasms, external causes of injury and poisoning and diseases of the respiratory diseases are given for all ages and for both sexes combined in Fig. 15–18.

Following a period of stagnation, mortality from circulatory diseases has been falling since 2000 at approximately the same pace as the regional and EU15 averages, resulting in the most recent rate 37% higher than the EU15 average. Cancer mortality is low and has remained unchanged since 2000, contrary to the reducing trends in Europe. The most recent rate is only 8% lower than the EU15 average.

Fig. 13. **Maternal deaths per 100 000 live births, three-year rolling average,** Greece, WHO European Region and EU15, 1980–2012

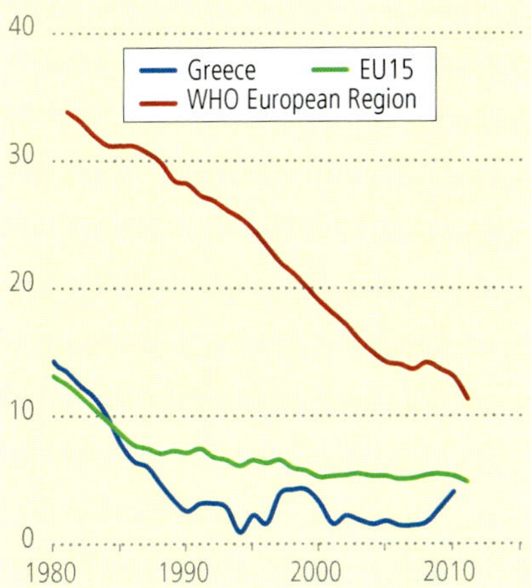

Fig. 14. **Mortality profile from main causes of death, age-standardized death rate per 100 000 population,** Greece, WHO European Region and EU15, 2011 or latest available year

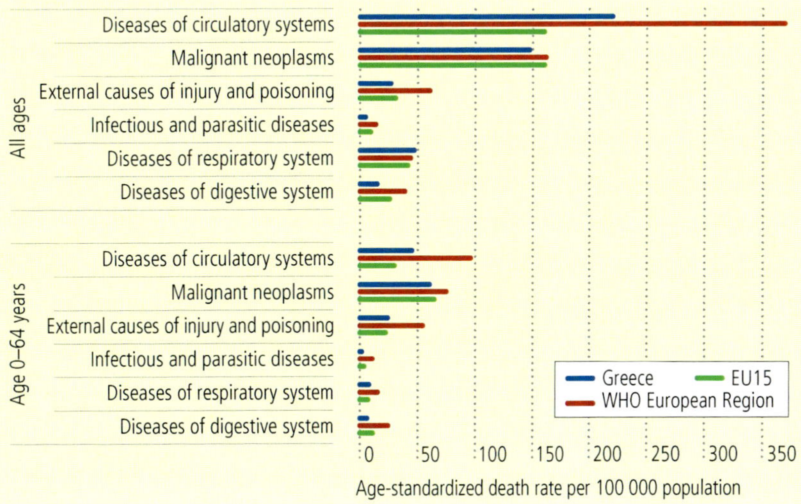

The age-standardized mortality rate from diseases of the respiratory system has remained steady since 2000 following an increasing trend in the previous decade. While the EU15 average has decreased for both males and females since 2000, the Greek rate has remained steady among the population aged 45 years or more, and has even increased for men and women aged 45–59 years and women aged 75 years or more. In 2011, the age-standardized mortality rate from diseases of the respiratory system for Greek males (54.7/100 000) remained slightly below the EU15 average (56.0/100 00). In contrast, the rate for Greek females (39.9/100 000) was more than one fourth higher than the EU15 average (31.2/100 000).

Fig. 15. **Age-standardized death rate from diseases of the circulatory system, all ages per 100 000 population,** Greece, WHO European Region and EU15, 1980–2011

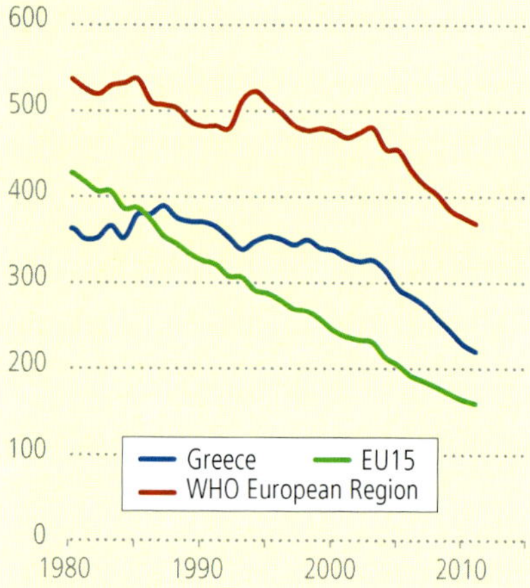

Other major causes of death

The age-standardized mortality rate from infectious diseases for all ages (Fig. 19) has remained at the same level, while the countries of the EU15 and the Region have faced increasing levels. In 2011, the age-standardized mortality rate (4.7/100 000) was clearly below the averages of the EU15 (8.8/100 000) and the Region (13.1/100 000).

The age-standardized mortality rate from diseases of the digestive system (Fig. 20) has decreased. The current rate in Greece (14.6/100 000) is substantially lower than the EU15 average (25.3/100 000) and the

Fig. 16. **Age-standardized death rate from malignant neoplasms, all ages per 100 000 population,** Greece, WHO European Region and EU15, 1980–2011

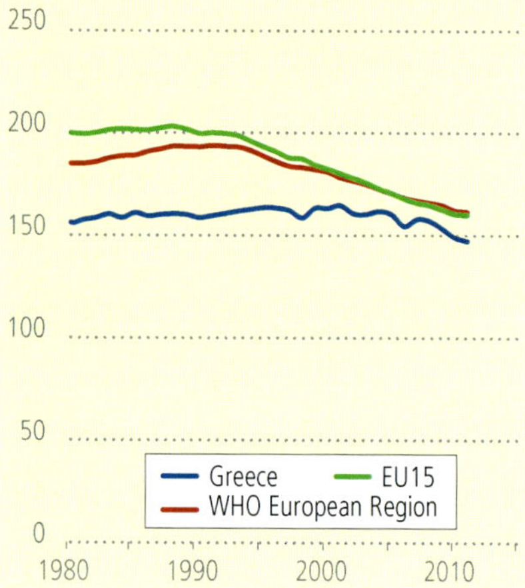

Fig. 17. **Age-standardized death rate from external causes of injury and poisoning, all ages per 100 000 population,** Greece, WHO European Region and EU15, 1980–2011

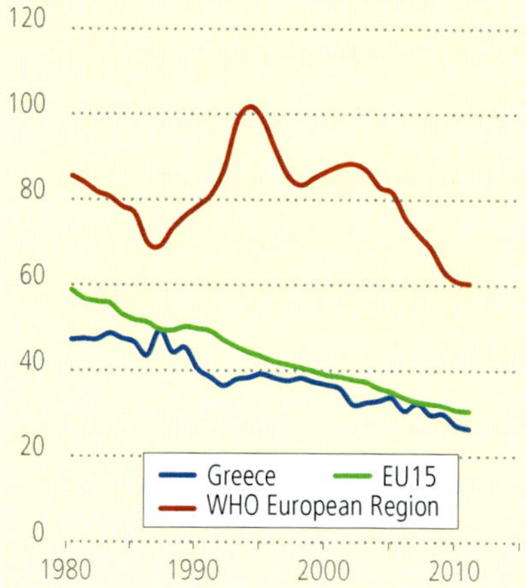

Fig. 18. **Age-standardized death rate from diseases of respiratory system, all ages per 100 000 population,** Greece, WHO European Region and EU15, 1980–2011

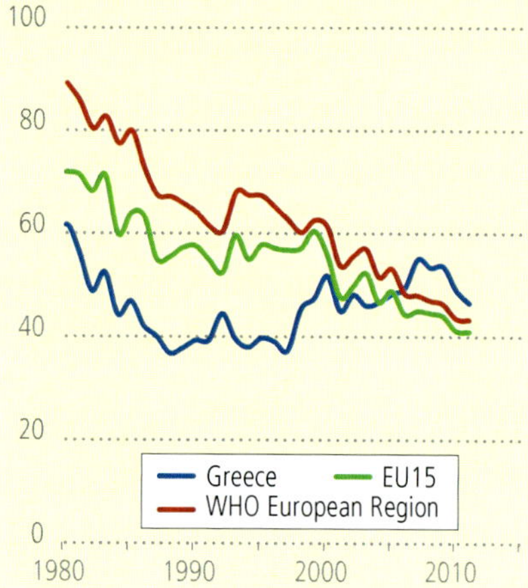

regional average (38.2/100 000). The trend is similar for deaths from chronic liver disease and cirrhosis, which together cause 44% of all deaths in this group in the Region. The share is lower in Greece (35%) as well as the EU15 countries on average (38%).

The suicide mortality rate in Greece has been among the lowest in the Region, with rates of 5 per 100 000 population for males and 1 per 100 000 population for females (Fig. 21, 22). The most recent rates from 2011 (6.2/100 000 for males and 1.3/100 000 for females) indicate increased mortality for both sexes (see Annex 2).

Similarly, the mortality from homicides and intentional injury for males almost doubled between 2006 and 2011 to a rate of 2.5 per 100 000. This is substantially higher than the EU15 average of below 1 per 100 000 population (Fig. 23). The rate for females has remained low in Greece (0.5/100 000 in 2011), level with the EU15 average (0.4/100 000) (Fig. 24).

The age-standardized mortality rate from motor vehicle accidents has halved in the last 15 years (Fig. 25, 26), but is still more than double the EU15 average indicating further room for improvement, especially for males. Specifically, the 2011 rate for Greek males was 17.1/100 000, higher than the average for the Region (14.6/100 000), while the mortality rates for females were equivalent for Greece (4.2/100 00) and the Region (4.3/100 000).

Fig. 19. **Age-standardized death rate from infectious and parasitic diseases, all ages per 100 000 population,** Greece, WHO European Region and EU15, 1980–2011

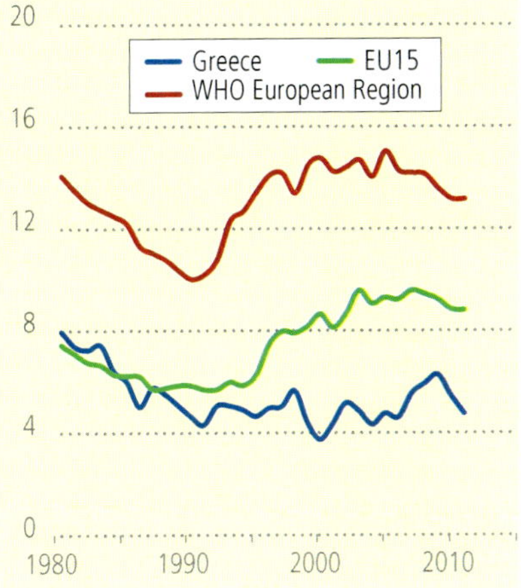

Fig. 20. **Age-standardized death rate from diseases of the digestive system, all ages per 100 000 population,** Greece, WHO European Region and EU15, 1980–2011

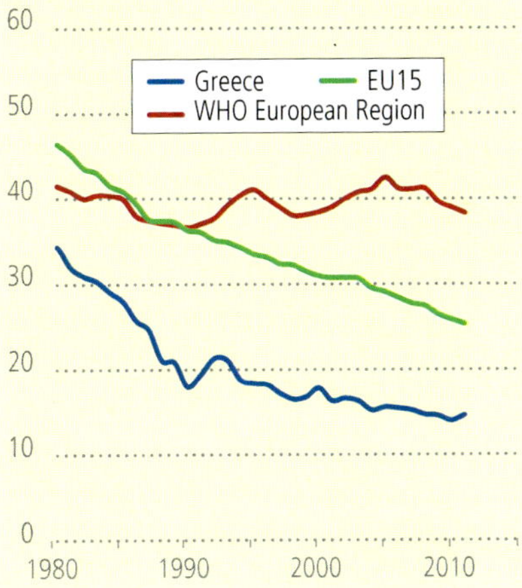

Fig. 21. **Age-standardized death rate from suicide and self-inflicted injury, all ages per 100 000 males,** Greece, WHO European Region and EU15, 1980–2011

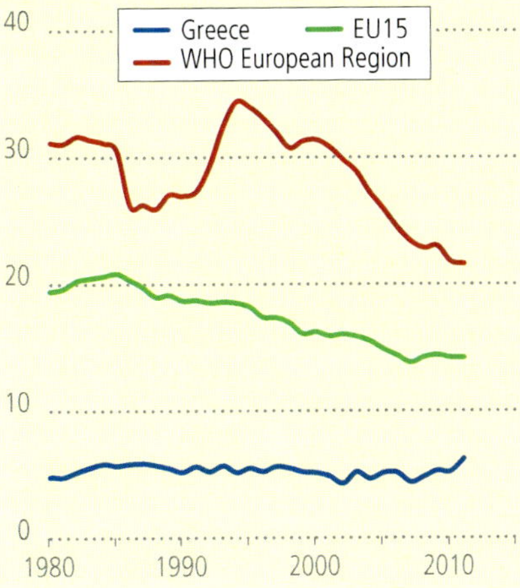

Fig. 22. **Age-standardized death rate from suicide and self-inflicted injury, all ages per 100 000 females,** Greece, WHO European Region and EU15, 1980–2011

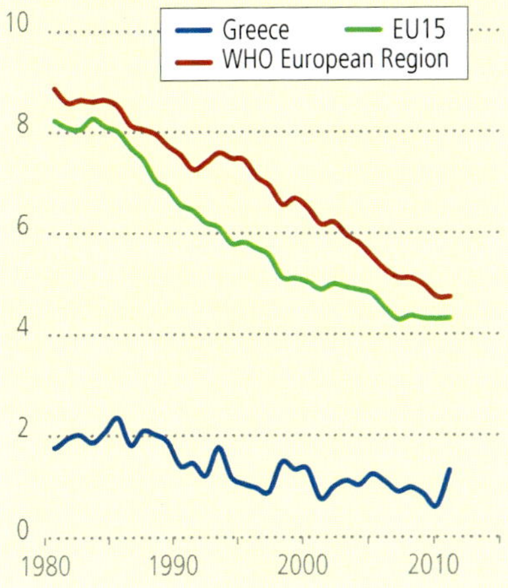

In addition to the trends highlighted in this section, selected causes of mortality are presented in Annex 2 comparing the percentage changes from 2000 to the latest available year in Greece (2011) with the averages for the Region (2011) and EU15 (2011).

Fig. 23. **Age-standardized death rate from homicide and intentional injury, all ages per 100 000 males,** Greece, WHO European Region and EU15, 1980–2011

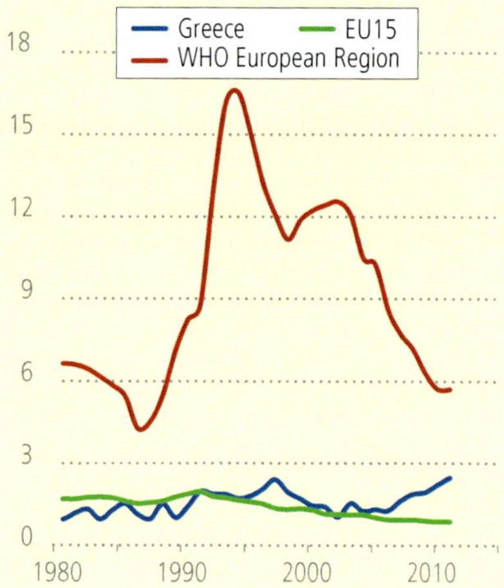

Premature mortality

As a considerable number of premature deaths from cardiovascular diseases, cancer and accidents are influenced by health-related behaviour and habits, trend analyses of premature mortality (defined as death under the age of 65 years) between countries can confirm which, if any, treatments and health promotion and prevention measures have been successfully implemented.

The premature mortality rate from diseases of the circulatory system has decreased in most European countries in the last decades. Since 2000, the premature mortality rate for both sexes combined has fallen by 18% in Greece, against an average decrease for the EU15 of 33%. Even though the age-standardized mortality rate for both sexes combined is, on average, double for the Region compared to Greece, the EU15 average is one third lower. In 2011, Greek males had a 60% higher premature mortality rate from diseases of the circulatory system than the average for the EU15, while the difference for Greek females was only 35% (Fig. 27, 28).

Fig. 24. **Age-standardized death rate from homicide and intentional injury, all ages per 100 000 females,** Greece, WHO European Region and EU15, 1980–2011

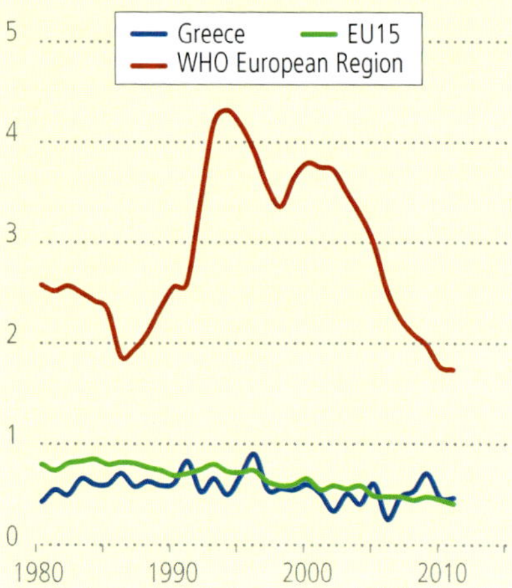

Fig. 25. **Age-standardized death rate from motor vehicle accidents, all ages per 100 000 males,** Greece, WHO European Region and EU15, 1980–2011

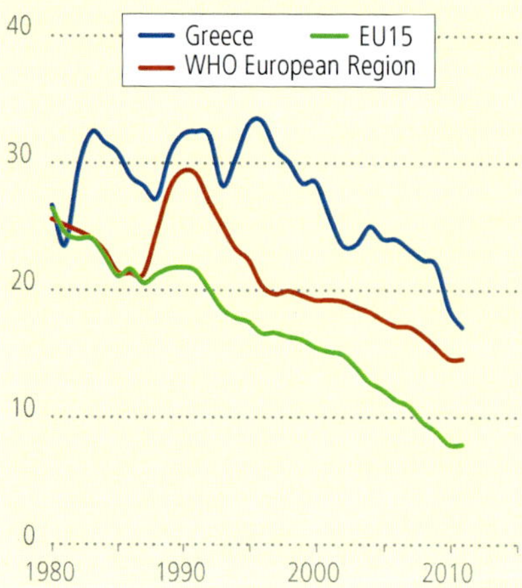

Fig. 26. **Age-standardized death rate from motor vehicle accidents, all ages per 100 000 females,** Greece, WHO European Region and EU15, 1980–2011

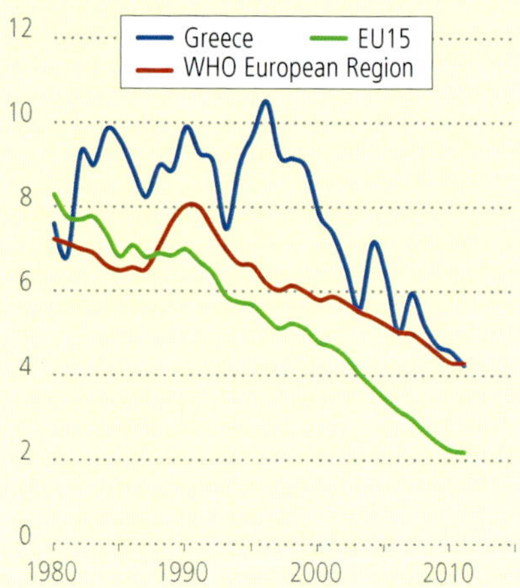

As with the diseases of the circulatory system, premature deaths from ischaemic heart disease for Greek males have been in decline since 2000, although to a lesser extent than in the EU15 (14%; Fig. 29). By 2011, the premature mortality rate from diseases of the circulatory system in Greece had decreased to 45/100 000, more than double the EU15 rate of 22/100 000. For women, the premature mortality rate from ischaemic heart disease was approximately 10/100 000 for decades with only minor annual variations (Fig. 30). The most recent rate for women in Greece (in 2011) was double the average rate of the EU15.

Fig. 27. **Age-standardized death rate from diseases of circulatory system, 0–64 years per 100 000 males,** Greece, WHO European Region and EU15, 1980–2011

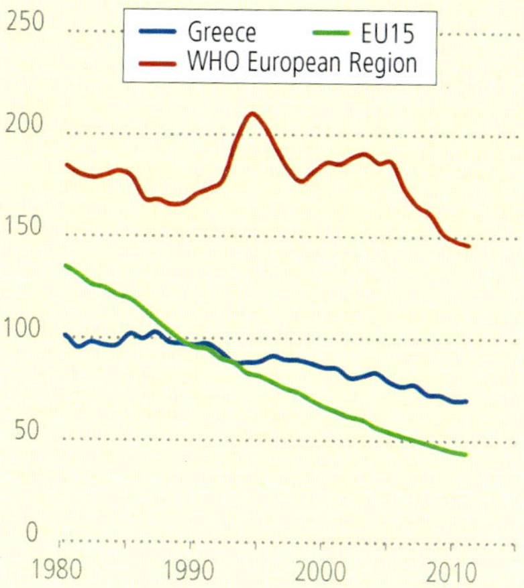

For premature deaths from cerebrovascular diseases, the mortality rate has decreased more slowly in Greece than in the EU15 on average, especially for males (Figs. 31, 32). The age-standardized mortality rate for males was 74% higher and for females 33% higher than the EU15 average in 2011.

The decline in premature mortality from malignant neoplasms began earlier in Greece than in the EU15 and the Region for both sexes. Reductions in the premature mortality rate since 2000 were, however, appreciably less in Greece than in the Region and the EU15. Between 2000 and 2011, the decline in Greece was 11% for men, while the EU15 and regional averages declined by at least by almost one fifth (Fig. 33). For females, the decline in Greece (5%) was only half the decline seen in the EU15 (12%) or the Region (11%) (Fig. 34). For men, the Greek rate (75/100 000)

Fig. 28. **Age-standardized death rate from diseases of circulatory system, 0–64 years per 100 000 females,** Greece, WHO European Region and EU15, 1980–2011

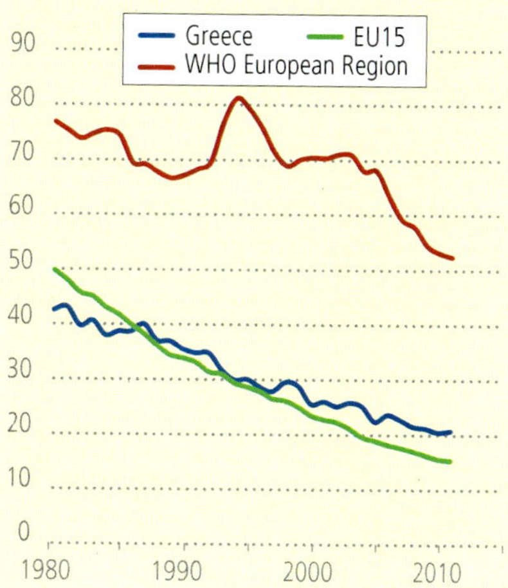

Fig. 29. **Age-standardized death rate from ischaemic heart disease, 0–64 years per 100 000 males,** Greece, WHO European Region and EU15, 1980–2011

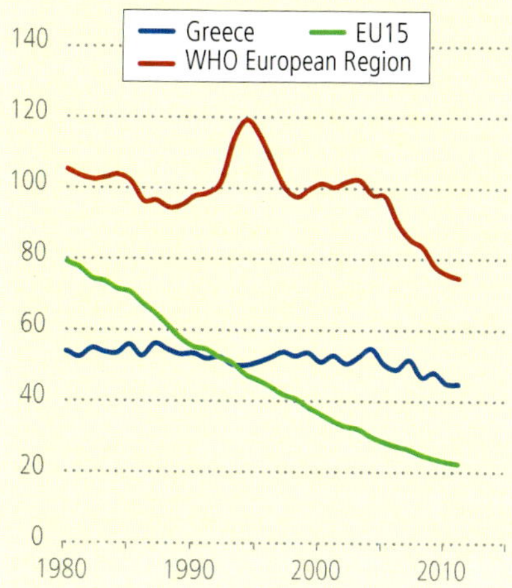

Fig. 30. **Age-standardized death rate from ischaemic heart disease, 0–64 years per 100 000 females,** Greece, WHO European Region and EU15, 1980–2011

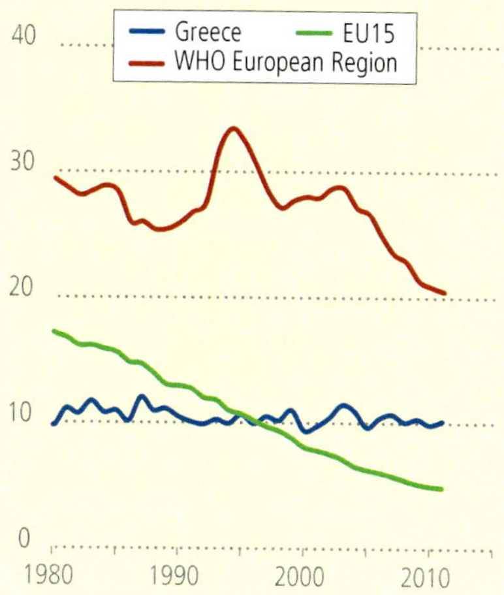

equals the EU15 average (74/100 000) but is lower than the average for the Region (91/100 000) (Fig. 33). Premature mortality for Greek women from malignant neoplasms is lower (46/100 000) than the averages for their counterparts in the EU15 (55/100 000) and the Region (61/100 000) (Fig. 34).

Fig. 31. **Age-standardized death rate for cerebrovascular diseases, 0–64 years per 100 000 males,** Greece, WHO European Region and EU15, 1980–2011

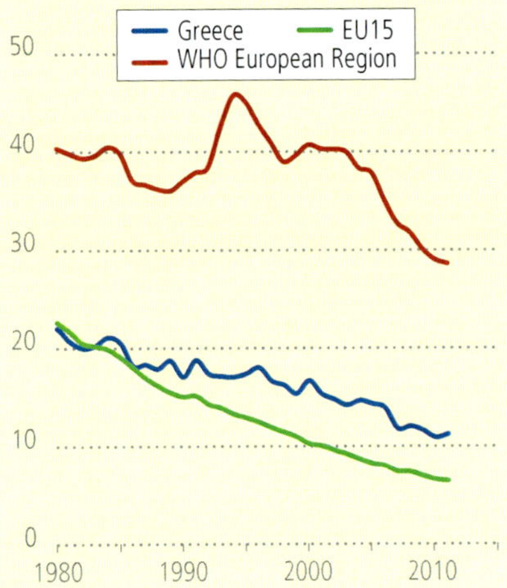

The premature mortality rate from trachea, bronchus and lung cancer for males has decreased by 14% in Greece since 2000, substantially less than the average decline in the EU15 (20%) and in the Region (23%) (Fig. 35). Consequently, the rate among Greek men in 2011 (29/100 000) was the highest among the EU15 after France, above the regional average of 26/100 000 (Fig. 35). For women, the premature mortality rate from trachea, bronchus and lung cancer in Greece has remained below the EU15 average (Fig. 36). Even though the rate has increased from 5/100 000 to 7/100 000, it is lower than the averages for the EU15 (10/100 000) and the Region (8/100 000).

The premature mortality rate from malignant neoplasm of the female breast has been below 15 per 100 000 women for decades (Fig. 37). In 2011 the rate remained 25–30% under the averages for the EU15 and the Region.

While the premature mortality rate from cancer of the cervix uteri has historically been low in Greece, the rate (1.5/100 000)

Fig. 32. **Age-standardized death rate for cerebrovascular disease, 0–64 years per 100 000 females,** Greece, WHO European Region and EU15, 1980–2011

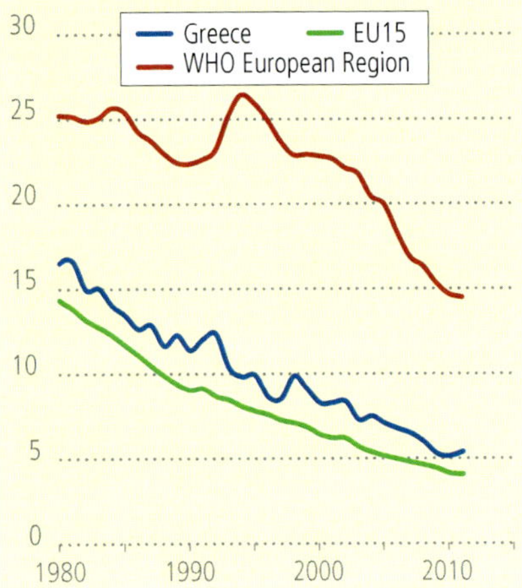

Fig. 33. **Age-standardized death rate from malignant neoplasms, 0–64 years per 100 000 males,** Greece, WHO European Region and EU15, 1980–2015

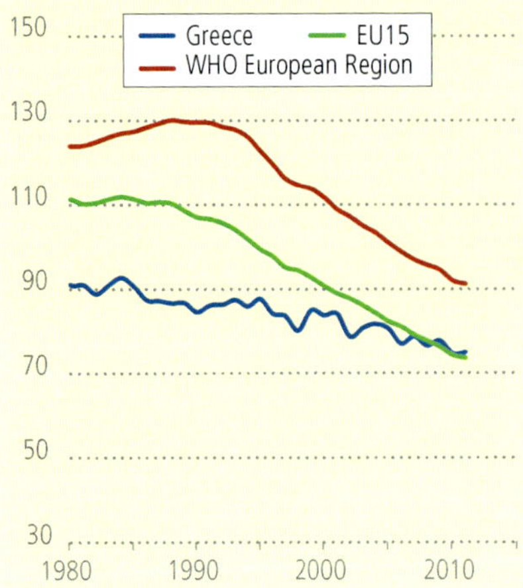

Fig. 34. **Age-standardized death rate from malignant neoplasms, 0–64 years per 100 000 females,** Greece, WHO European Region and EU15, 1980–2011

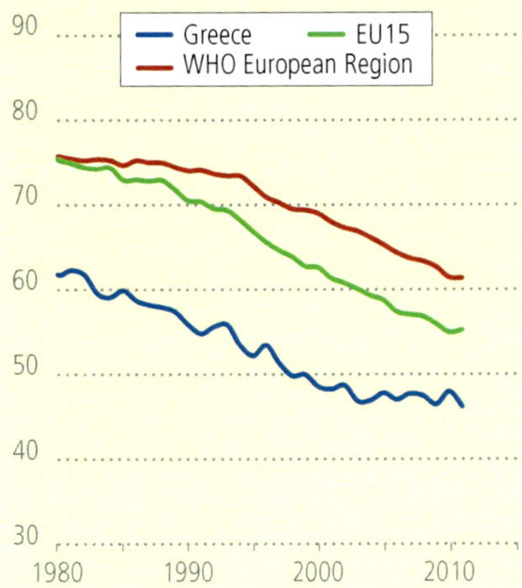

has increased since the mid-2000s to the same level as the EU15 average, although still well below the average for the Region (Fig. 38). Specifically, the increase is largest for women aged 45–59 years.

Fig. 35. **Age-standardized death rate from trachea, bronchus and lung cancer, 0–64 years per 100 000 males,** Greece, WHO European Region and EU15, 1980–2011

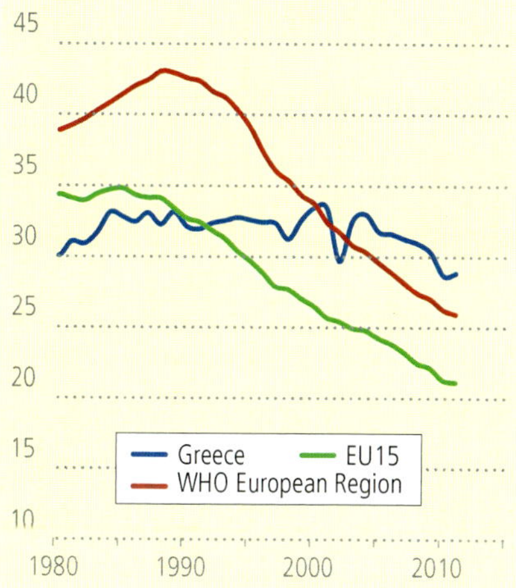

Fig. 36. **Age-standardized death rate from trachea, bronchus and lung cancer, 0–64 years per 100 000 females,** Greece, WHO European Region and EU15, 1980–2011

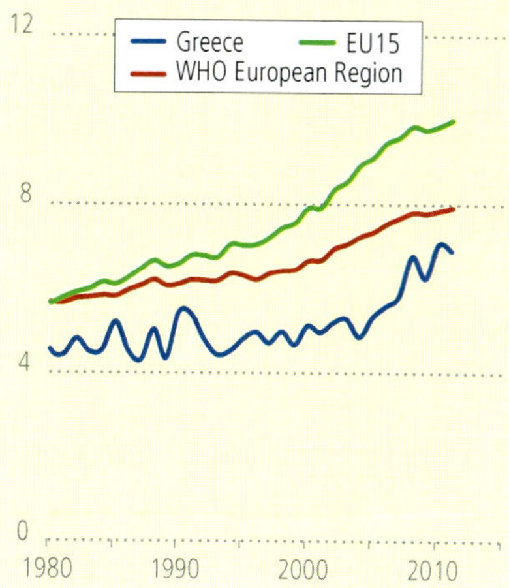

Fig. 37. **Age-standardized death rate from female breast cancer, 0–64 years per 100 000 females,** Greece, WHO European Region and EU15, 1980–2011

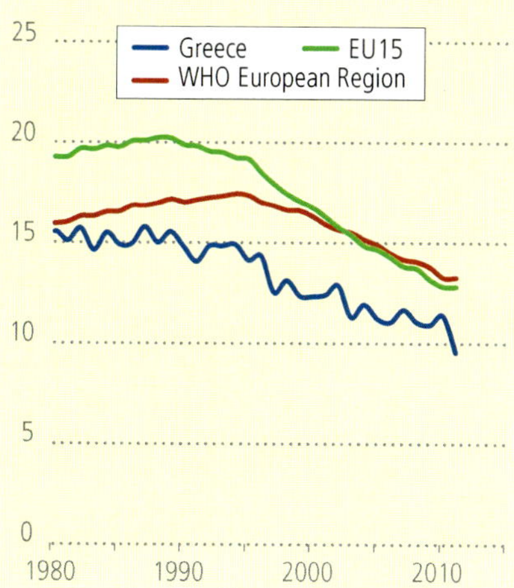

Fig. 38. **Age-standardized death rate from cancer of the cervix uteri, 0–64 years per 100 000 females,** Greece, WHO European Region and EU15, 1980–2011

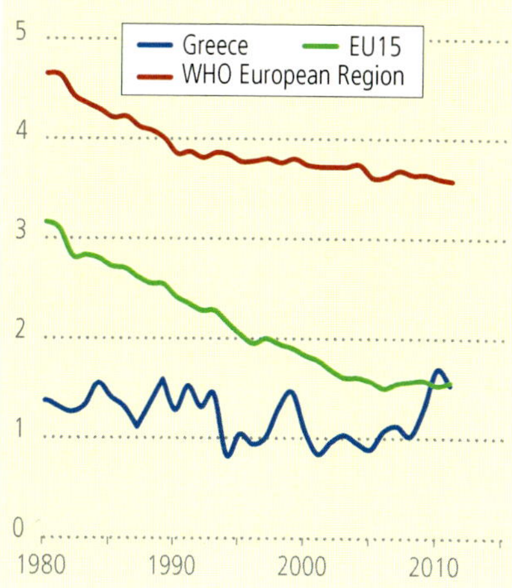

Risk factors and determinants of health

Several factors, including genetics, physical and social environments and health behaviour, affect the health and well-being of individuals and the population. Risk factors such as unhealthy diets, low physical activity, smoking and heavy alcohol consumption are linked to elevated blood pressure, high serum cholesterol and overweight. These risk factors contribute to premature mortality from cardiovascular diseases and cancers in particular, the two main causes of death in Europe. Risk factors also contribute to a wide range of other chronic illnesses and thus affect the quality of life in general.

Alcohol consumption

The consumption of alcohol is measured as the recorded amount of alcohol consumed per adult aged 15 years or more over a calendar year in a country, in litres of pure (100%) alcohol. The recorded alcohol consumption per capita for the adult population in Greece decreased over the last three decades to a record low of 7.9 litres per capita in 2010 (Fig. 39). This is lower than the averages for the Region (9.8 litres) and the EU15 (9.9 litres). These sales figures do not cover unrecorded consumption, which is estimated to be moderate at two litres per capita *(7)*.

Fig. 39. **Pure alcohol consumption, recorded litres per capita, adults aged 15+ years**, Greece, WHO European Region and EU15, 1980–2010

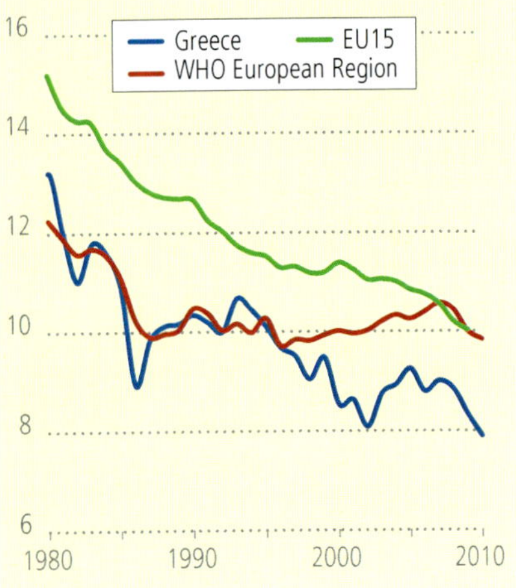

Tobacco smoking

The percentage of regular daily smokers is measured among adults aged 15 years and older. In Greece the smoking rates are very high for both sexes. The prevalence of daily smoking among Greek males in 2013 was 49.7, according to the latest Global Adult Tobacco Survey for Greece *(9)*, indicating an increase of almost three percentage points since 2000. Among Greek males aged 25–44 years, 63.2% were regular daily smokers. While the prevalence among Greek females declined from 29% in 2000 to 23.9% in 2013, the rates remain high compared to both the Region and the EU15, where smoking levels are continuously decreasing (Fig. 40). Of current daily smokers aged 15 years and over, Greek males smoked an average of 21 cigarettes per day, while females smoked an average of 17.

Diet, consumption of macronutrients and overweight

While the average number of calories available per person per day has increased by around 100 kcal per decade in Greece, it has remained within a steady range since 2000. In 2009, the average Greek had 3661 kcal available per day, 5% higher than the EU15 and regional averages. In Greece, 38% of total energy came from fat, similar to the averages for the EU15 (39%) and the Region (36%). The average number of fruits and vegetables available per person per year in Greece (386 kg) is among the highest in the Region, more than 50% higher than the averages for the EU15 (231 kg) and the Region (243 kg).

WHO estimates that in 2014, 66% of men and 55% of women in Greece were overweight (body mass index ≥25), with an increase of two percentage points since 2010 for both sexes *(7)*. In addition, the prevalence of obesity (body mass index of ≥30) increased by two percentage points. In 2014, Greek women were more likely to be obese (24%) than men (22%). The averages for the Region are similar to that in Greece regarding the share of overweight women (55%) and the share of obesity for both men (21%) and women (25%). Greek men, however, have a much higher likelihood (four percentage points) of being overweight than their regional counterparts.

Fig. 40. **Percentage of regular daily smokers in the population aged 15+ years,** Greece, WHO European Region and EU15, 1980–2013

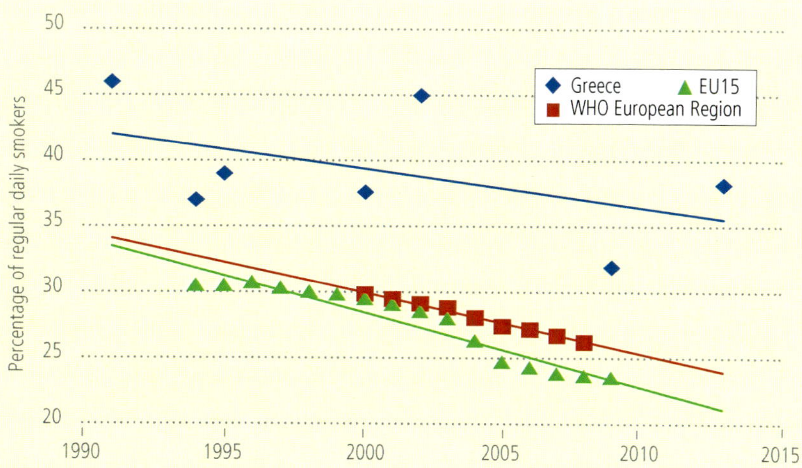

Comparative risk assessment

WHO has produced estimates for the number of disability-adjusted life years attributable to selected risk factors at regional level, but not at country level. The estimates produced by the Institute for Health Metrics and Evaluation are, therefore, used in this publication since they are available at country level *(10)*. The Institute estimates that the highest burden of disease in Greece is caused by tobacco smoking, followed by high blood pressure and dietary risks. Estimates from 2013 of the top 10 risk factors and the associated burden of disease measured in disability-adjusted life-years for Greece are given in Table 2, disaggregated by sex.

Table 2. **Top 10 risk factors and associated burden of disease,** age-standardized disability-adjusted life-years, 2013

Risk factors	Disability-adjusted life-years (average rate per 100 000 population)
Female	
High systolic blood pressure	3726
High body-mass index	2948
Dietary risks	2765
Tobacco smoke	2194
High fasting plasma glucose	1980
Low glomerular filtration rate	1613
High total cholesterol	1345
Low physical activity	1074
Air pollution	793
Alcohol and drug use	518
Male	
Tobacco smoke	6193
High systolic blood pressure	4525
Dietary risks	4229
High body-mass index	3344
High fasting plasma glucose	2147
Alcohol and drug use	2135
High total cholesterol	2103
Low glomerular filtration rate	1416
Air pollution	1322
Low physical activity	1164

Source: Institute for Health Metrics and Evaluation *(10)*.

Health system

The key indicators for the health system in 2013 are shown in Table 3. The number of hospital beds was 5% below the EU15 average and 27% lower than the average for the Region. As regards human health resources, the levels had been increasing for physicians, dentists, nurses and midwives since 2000. The availability of physicians and dentists per capita was much higher than the EU15 average (+67% and +80%, respectively), while the numbers of nurses and midwives per capita were well below the EU15 average (-59% and -27%, respectively).

The number of inpatient care discharges rose from 16.1 per 100 in 2000 to 19.8 per 100 in 2008 (latest available data). This rate was higher than the averages for the EU15 (16.8/100) and the Region (17.9/100). The average length of stay in all hospitals has shown a steady decrease. The most recent rate (6.6 days in 2008) was two to three days shorter than the averages for the EU15 (9.2 days in 2011) and the Region (9.5 days in 2011).

Table 3. **Key indicators on health resources, use of health services and health expenditure,** 2013 or latest available

Indicators	Greece	Change since 2000	WHO European Region	EU15
Hospital beds per 100 000 population	484.9	3%	665.4	508.1
Physicians per 100 000 population	614.5	42%	333.8	368.2
Dentists per 100 000 population	128.5	13%	42.5	71.3
Nurses per 100 000 population	353.9	21%	765.9	868.4
Midwives per 100 000 population	23.3	12%	43.5	31.7
Inpatient care discharges per 100 population	19.8	23%	17.9	16.8
Average length of stay, all hospitals	6.6	-21%	9.5	9.2
Outpatient contacts per person per year	4	-8%	7.7	6.9
Total health expenditure as % of GDP[a]	9.8	1.9[b]	8.2	10.3
Total health expenditure, PPP$ per capita[a]	2513	73%	2455	3871
Public sector health expenditure as % of total health expenditure[a]	69.5	9.5[b]	67.2	77.1
Out-of-pocket health expenditure as % of total health expenditure[a]	26.4	-8[b]	26.3	14.2

[a] WHO estimates.
[b] Change in percentage points.

The average number of outpatient contacts has remained unchanged for decades. The most recent available average is from 2006 (4.0), lower than those for the EU15 (6.9 in 2011) and for the Region (7.7 in 2011).

WHO's estimate for health expenditure shows that the share of GDP increased from 7.9% in 2000 to 10.1% in 2008 and then decreased to 9.8% in 2013. This was higher than the average for the Region (8.2% in 2013) but lower than the EU15 average (10.3% in 2013). Total health expenditure, adjusted by PPP per capita, more than doubled from US$ 1454 in 2000 to US$ 3013 in 2008 but decreased by one fifth after the economic crisis began. The rate in 2013 (US$ 2513) equalled the rate in 2006, remaining just above the average for the Region but 35% lower than the EU15 average. The most recent (2013) WHO estimate of public sector health expenditure was 69.5% of total spending on health, just below the average for the Region (67.2%) but eight percentage points below the EU15 average (77.1%). Although out-of-pocket expenditure decreased by eight percentage points between 2000 and 2013, it was still almost twice as high as the EU15 average. The unmet need for health care increased from 3.1% in 2004 to 7.8% in 2013 *(11)*. Following the economic crisis, public sector expenditure on health as a percentage of total government expenditure decreased by 1.3 percentage points after 2009 to 11.7% in 2013.

A detailed description of the health system in Greece in 2010 is given in *Greece: health system review (12)*.

Health 2020

As stated in the Introduction, Health 2020 is the health policy of the WHO European Region, which aims to support action across government and society to significantly improve the health and well-being of populations, reduce health inequalities, strengthen public health and ensure people-centred health systems that are universal, equitable, sustainable and of high quality *(2)*. European Member States have agreed on a set of core indicators to monitor the progress on Health 2020 policy targets in the Region and in all Member States *(3)*.

The newly revised highlights on health and well-being and accompanying profiles on Hhealth and well-Being publications constitute a country-by-country means of reporting progress towards achieving the overarching targets of Health 2020. For Greece, the Health 2020 indicators are given in Table 4.

Reduce premature mortality by 2020

Since 2000, Greece has made headway in reducing premature mortality (defined as mortality among those aged 30–69 years), although progress is slight and not uniform across all indicators. Regarding the four selected major noncommunicable diseases (cardiovascular diseases, cancer, diabetes mellitus and chronic respiratory diseases), the age-standardized overall premature mortality rate combined declined annually by 1.6% between 2000 and 2013 for both sexes. While this decline was on a par with the regional target of 1.5% per year, the Region as a whole and the comparative EU15 regions achieved substantially greater gains during the same period. Although premature mortality from digestive diseases fell by only 0.1% annually between 2000 and 2013, the levels are very low. The prevalence of tobacco smoking and overweight and obesity remain very high, contributing to the high premature mortality from noncommunicable diseases. On the other hand, recorded alcohol consumption is low and decreasing, which is reflected in the low mortality rate from diseases of the digestive system.

Spurred by outbreaks of rubella in the 1990s *(12)*, the authorities have implemented the measles/mumps/rubella vaccine to the extent that in 2012, 99% of children were vaccinated compared to 95% in the Region and 93% in the EU15. In parallel, the child immunization rate for poliomyelitis increased from 89% in 2000 to 99% in 2012, again higher than in the Region and the EU15. Thus Greece appears within range of realizing the Health 2020 target for achieving and sustaining the elimination of poliomyelitis, measles and rubella.

Table 4. **Core indicators for monitoring Health 2020 policy targets in Greece,** most recent years available

Target	Indicator	Value			Year
		Male	Female	Total	
1. Reduce premature mortality[a]	Premature mortality rate from cardiovascular disease, cancer, diabetes mellitus and chronic respiratory diseases among people aged 30 to under 70 years	365	161	259	2011
	Prevalence of tobacco use among adults aged 18 years and over[b] *(5)*	51.2	25.7	38.2	2013
	Pure alcohol consumption per capita among adults aged 15 years and over	–	–	7.4	2011
	Prevalence of overweight and obese (body mass index ≥25) adults aged 18 years and over (age-standardized estimate) *(6)*	66	55	61	2014
	Mortality rate from external causes of injury and poisoning, all ages	42	11	26	2011
2. Increase life expectancy	Life expectancy at birth, in years	78.6	83.2	80.9	2011
3. Reduce inequities[c]	Infant mortality rate per 1000 live births	3.2	2.6	2.9	2012
	Proportion of children of official primary school age not enrolled (net enrolment rate *(7)*)	0.8	0.2	0.5	2011
	Unemployment *(8)*	23.6	30.2	26.5	2014
	National policy addressing reduction of health inequities established and documented	NA	NA	No	NA
	Gini coefficient *(9)*	–	–	0.37	2012
4. Enhance well-being[d]	Life satisfaction among adults aged 15 years and older *(10)*	–	–	5.1	2007–2012
	Availability of social support among adults aged 50 years and older *(10)*	–	–	61	2013
	Percentage of population with improved sanitation facilities *(11)*	–	–	99	2015
5. Universal coverage and "right to health"	Private household out-of-pocket expenditure as proportion of total health expenditure	NA	NA	26.4	2013
	Percentage of children vaccinated against measles (one dose by second birthday)	–	–	99	2012
	Percentage of children vaccinated against poliomyelitis (three doses by first birthday)	–	–	99	2012
	Percentage of children vaccinated against rubella (one dose by second birthday)	–	–	99	2012
	Total health expenditure as a percentage of gross domestic product	NA	NA	9.8	2013
6. National targets	Establishment of process for target-setting documented	NA	NA	No	2015
	Evidence documenting:				
	(a) national health service aligned with Health 2020	NA	NA	No	2015
	(b) implementation plan	NA	NA	No	2015
	(c) accountability mechanism	NA	NA	No	2015

NA: not applicable.
[a] Target 1 includes percentage of children vaccinated against measles, poliomyelitis and rubella.
[b] Prevalence includes both daily and occasional (less than daily) use among adults aged 15 years or more.
[c] Target 3 includes life expectancy at birth.
[d] Target 4 includes Gini coefficient, the unemployment rate and the proportion of children not enrolled in primary school.
Source: WHO European Health for All database *(4)* unless otherwise specified.

Increase life expectancy

Life expectancy at birth was 78.6 years for males and 83.2 years for females in 2011, representing an increase by 3.0 years for males and 2.4 years for females since 2000. So far, the 2011 figures illustrate that life expectancy is increasing adequately at the current rates,[3] disaggregated for males and females, as per the Health 2020 target.

Reduce inequalities in health

With regard to children, Greece has gained significant ground in rectifying gaps in health status associated with social determinants. As of 2011, infant mortality rates were 3.6/1000 live births for boys and 3.1/1000 live births for girls, representing a decrease of 41% for boys and 35% for girls since 2000. For both sexes, infant mortality rates are lower than the EU15 average and substantially lower than the regional average. Improvements have also been made in the proportion of children of official primary school age not enrolled, which had fallen to 0.8% for boys and 0.2% for girls by 2011 *(13)*. Encouragingly, this represented a decline of almost 90% between 2000 and 2012 for both sexes combined, the most recent year for which non-disaggregated data are available *(13)*.

Unemployment is a priority area in the Health 2020 targets *(1)*. As a consequence of the economic crisis, unemployment rates rose substantially in Greece. In 2014, the rates were 23.6% for males, representing an increase of 16.2 percentage points since 2000, and 30.2% for females, representing an increase of 13.2 percentage points since 2000 *(6)*. Unemployment among those aged 15–19 years was 61.8% in 2014, an increase of 24.7 percentage points since 2000. As a measure of income distribution or consumption expenditure, the Gini index for 2012 was 0.37, an increase of 0.03 since 2004 *(14)*. When taken together, the increases both in unemployment and the Gini index underline the need for a policy to bring about a reduction in health inequalities.

Enhance the well-being of the population

Well-being, as monitored by a suite of indicators, is a relatively new construct and thus will require further country data before an adequate trend analysis may be performed. Data from the United Nations Development Programme's Human Development Index for

[3] The annual rate during 2006–2010.

the years 2007–2012 give an overall life satisfaction index for Greece of 5.1 on a scale from 0 (least satisfied) to 10 (most satisfied) *(17)*, lower than the average for the EU15 (6.7) and the Region (6.0) *(17)*. In 2013, 61% of people aged over 50 years reported that they had relatives or friends on whom they could count when in trouble, among the lowest of such figures in the Region and well below the averages for the EU15 (90%) and the Region (85%). The percentage of the population with improved water and sanitation facilities has risen and is nearly universal according to 2015 data from the WHO/United Nations Children's Fund Joint Monitoring Programme *(16)*. As of 2015, 100% of homes, both rural and urban, had a piped drinking water supply, and 98% of rural populations and 99% of urban populations had access to a sewerage system, septic tank or other hygienic means of sewage disposal.

Ensure universal coverage and the right to the highest attainable level of health

The health system has undergone substantive changes following the economic crisis in 2009. As many of these reforms are ongoing, WHO's estimates from 2013 do not fully reflect the current status of health expenditure in Greece. The proportion of private households' out-of-pocket expenditure was 26.4% in 2013, representing a decrease of eight percentage points since 2000. This was still well beyond the threshold of 15% required to prevent significant catastrophic health expenditure and almost twice as high as the EU15 average. As the unmet need for medical care almost doubled from 4.0% in 2009 to 7.8% in 2013 *(11)*, the decrease in out-of-pocket expenditure was probably a reflection of economic hardship. According to WHO estimates, the total expenditure on health (as a percentage of GDP) increased by two percentage points to 9.8% between 2000 and 2013. This increase was, however, due to the decrease in GDP, as total health expenditure in purchasing power parities decreased by 22% between 2009 and 2012.

Set national goals and targets related to health

By 2015, Greece had initiated the development of a national reform plan for the health sector, focusing on structural reforms of the health care delivery model, its financing and governance with a view to moving towards universal health coverage. The document has not, however, been formally adopted yet.

Conclusions

This publication presents the health situation and trends analysis for Greece. Historically, the Greek population has been one of the healthiest in Europe. Although the health status of the Greek population has in general steadily improved over time, the improvements have been slower than in other EU15 countries and most recent data indicate that the situation is in line with or worse than the average EU15 situation.

Life expectancy is no exception. In 2011, life expectancy for men (78.6 years) equalled the EU15 average, while the figure for women (83.2 years) was almost one year lower than the EU15 average. Healthy life expectancy increased by two years to 69 years for men and by four years to 73 years for women between 2000 and 2013.

Deaths from diseases of the circulatory system, malignant neoplasms (cancers) and external causes of injury and poisoning (accidents, suicides and homicides) are the main killers in the Region. In Greece, they caused 72% of all deaths in 2011. The age-standardized mortality rates from infectious diseases and diseases of the digestive system have remained below the EU15 average. The mortality rate from diseases of the respiratory system, however, increased in the late 1990s although it has stagnated since then, especially among men and women aged 45 years or more. The mortality rate from external causes and poisonings is less than half of the average for the Region. The suicide mortality rate is still among the lowest in the Region, even though it increased in 2011. Mortality from homicides and intentional injury for males almost doubled between 2006 and 2011 to 2.5 per 100 000 population, while the rate for females remained low. Mortality from motor vehicle accidents is more than double the EU15 average and, for males, above the regional average.

Although premature mortality before the age of 65 years is relatively high compared to the EU15 countries, it is still well below the regional averages. Compared to the EU15 averages, premature mortality from diseases of the circulatory system in 2011 was 60% higher for males and 35% higher for females. For ischaemic heart disease, the mortality rates are double the EU15 average for both sexes, while for cerebrovascular diseases the Greek rate is 74% higher for males and 33% higher for females. Premature cancer mortality started to decrease sooner in Greece than elsewhere in Europe but more slowly, so that the most recent figures are almost in line with EU15 averages. Premature mortality from trachea, bronchus and lung cancer for males is among the highest in the EU15. Greece is on track to reach the regional target level defined by WHO *(3)* for reducing premature mortality from four major noncommunicable diseases (cardiovascular diseases, cancer, diabetes mellitus and chronic respiratory diseases) but not for the diseases of the digestive system.

Greece is one of only two counties in Europe to continue using the outdated ninth revision of the International Classification of Diseases, which further limits the comparability and usability of cause of death data. The quality of cause of death data is also of concern, as 11% of deaths in 2011 were assigned to ill-defined causes, the highest proportion among all EU15 countries.

Reported alcohol consumption has decreased from very high levels to 7.9 litres per capita per year in 2010, around two litres less than in the EU15 and the Region on average. The prevalences of tobacco smoking and of overweight and obesity are very high.

The reported incidences of most infectious diseases are below the averages for the EU15 and the Region, but the incidence of HIV has increased substantially in Greece since 2000, reaching a record high in 2012 of 10.7 per 100 000. In 2012, the incidences of HIV and AIDS were higher than the EU15 average but below the average for the Region. The vaccination rates are very high.

Although the density of physicians is one of the highest in Europe, most of them are specialists and concentrated in urban areas. The density of nurses, on the other hand, is very low: the lowest nurse to physician ratio in Europe is observed in Greece. Until the economic crisis hit Greece in 2009, total health expenditure as a percentage of GDP was in line with the EU15 average but it has decreased substantially since then. The major challenge is the high share of private expenditure. Out-of-pocket expenditure is the second highest in the EU15 and informal payments are widespread *(12)*.

The socioeconomic consequences of the 2009 economic crisis have been particularly devastating in Greece. The health status of the population has worsened, and there has been an increase in both maternal and infant mortality and the number of suicides and HIV cases, although the rates remain low compared to the averages for the Region. The economic crisis has also prompted a restructuring of the health system, which will have direct and indirect implications for health.

The recent increase in unemployment has resulted in one fifth of the population not being covered by health insurance *(18)*. The Gini index has increased, indicating a widening gap in income distribution. Life satisfaction, a measure of subjective well-being, is lower in Greece than the averages for the Region and the EU15. Among objective well-being measures, only 61% of people aged over 50 years reported that they had relatives or friends on whom they could count when in trouble, among the lowest proportions in the Region.

As a result of the ongoing economic crisis, the widening gap in health status compared to the EU15 and the absence of national health policies aligned with Health 2020, it is likely that inequalities will increase in comparison with the EU15 and that progress towards and achievement of Health 2020 goals might be jeopardized unless decisive proactive measures are taken soon.

References

1. Health 2020: a European policy framework supporting action across government and society for health and well-being. Copenhagen: WHO Regional Office for Europe; 2012 (EUR/RC62/9; http://www.euro.who.int/en/about-us/governance/regional-committee-for-europe/past-sessions/sixty-second-session/documentation/working-documents/eurrc629-health-2020-a-european-policy-framework-supporting-action-across-government-and-society-for-health-and-well-being, accessed 15 December 2015).
2. Health 2020: a European policy framework and strategy for the 21st century [website]. Copenhagen: WHO Regional Office for Europe; 2013 (http://www.euro.who.int/en/publications/policy-documents/health-2020.-a-european-policy-framework-and-strategy-for-the-21st-century-2013, accessed 12 March 2016).
3. Targets and indicators for Health 2020: Version 2. Copenhagen: WHO Regional Office for Europe; 2014 (http://www.euro.who.int/__data/assets/pdf_file/0009/251775/Health-2020-Targets-and-indicators-version2-ENG.pdf?ua=1, accessed 15 December 2015).
4. European Health for All database (HFA-DB) [online database]. Copenhagen: WHO Regional Office for Europe; 2015 (http://data.euro.who.int/hfadb/, accessed 15 December 2015).
5. Eurostat [online database]. Luxembourg: European Commission; 2016 (http://ec.europa.eu/eurostat/data/database, accessed 25 August 2015).
6. ILOSTAT database [online database]. Geneva: International Labour Organization; 2016 (http://www.ilo.org/ilostat/faces/help_home/data_by_country/country-details?_adf.ctrl-state=3wmg83w82_25&_afrLoop=552577240791405, accessed 12 March 2016).
7. Global Health Observatory (GHO) data [online database]. Geneva: World Health Organization; 2015 (http://www.who.int/gho/en/, accessed 12 March 2016).
8. International Classification of Diseases (ICD) [website]. Geneva: World Health Organization; 2016 (http://www.who.int/classifications/icd/en/, accessed 23 March 2016).
9. Global Adult Tobacco Survey: Greece 2013. Copenhagen: WHO Regional Office for Europe; 2015 (http://www.who.int/tobacco/surveillance/survey/gats/grc/en/, accessed 13 December 2015).
10. GBD Compare [online database]. Global Burden of Disease Study 2013 (GBD 2013). Results by risk factor 1990–2013. Seattle (WA):

Institute for Health Metrics and Evaluation; 2015 (http://ihmeuw.org/3si9, accessed 5 April 2016).
11. Self-reported unmet needs for medical care due to being too expensive, by income quintile [online database]. Luxembourg: Eurostat; 2016 (http://ec.europa.eu/eurostat/tgm/table.do?tab=table&plugin=1&language=en&pcode=tsdph270, accessed 12 March 2016).
12. Economou C. Greece: health system review. Health Syst. Transit. 2010;12(7):1–180.
13. UIS.STAT [online database]. Montreal: UNESCO Institute for Statistics; 2016 (http://www.uis.unesco.org/Pages/default.aspx, accessed 12 March 2016).
14. GINI index (World Bank estimate) [online database]. Washington (DC): World Bank; 2016 (http://data.worldbank.org/indicator/SI.POV.GINI, accessed 12 March 2016).
15. UNDP human development reports. Human Development Index (HDI) [website]. New York (NY): United Nations Development Programme; 2016 (http://hdr.undp.org/en/content/human-development-index-hdi, accessed 12 March 2016).
16. WHO/UNICEF Joint Monitoring Programme (JMP) for Water Supply and Sanitation [online database]. Geneva: World Health Organization; 2015 (http://www.wssinfo.org/, accessed 15 December 2015).
17. Gioula G, Fylaktou A, Exindari M, Atmatzidis G, Chatzidimitriou D, Melidou A et al. Rubella immunity and vaccination coverage of the population of northern Greece in 2006. Euro Surveill. 2007;12(11) (http://www.eurosurveillance.org/ViewArticle.aspx?ArticleId=747, accessed 23 March 2016).
18. Economou C, Kaitelidou D, Kentikelenis A, Maresso A, Sisouras A. The impact of the crisis on the health system and health in Greece. In: Maresso A, Mladovsky P, Thomson S, Sagan A, Karanikolos M, Richardson E et al., editors. Economic crisis, health systems and health in Europe. Country experience. Copenhagen: WHO Regional Office for Europe; 2015 (Observatory Studies Series No. 41; http://www.euro.who.int/__data/assets/pdf_file/0010/279820/Web-economic-crisis-health-systems-and-health-web.pdf?ua=1, accessed 12 March 2016).

Annex 1. ICD-10 codes for causes of death

Cause of death	ICD-10 codes
Cancer of cervix uteri	C53
Cancer of female breast	C50
Cancer of trachea, bronchus and lung	C33–C34
Cerebrovascular diseases	I60–I69
Chronic liver disease and cirrhosis	K70, K73, K74, K76
Diseases of the circulatory system	I00–I99
Diseases of the digestive system	K00–K93
Diseases of the respiratory system	J00–J99
External causes of injury and poisoning	V00–V99, W00–W99, X00–X99, Y00–Y99
Homicide and intentional injury	X85–X99, Y00–Y09
Infectious and parasitic disease	A00–A99, B00–B99
Ischaemic heart disease	I20–I25
Malignant neoplasms	C00–C97
Motor vehicle traffic accidents	V02–V04, V09, V12–V14, V20–V79, V82, V87, V89
Suicide and self-inflicted injury	X60–X84
Symptoms, signs and ill-defined conditions	R00-R53, R55-R99
Tuberculosis	A15–A19, B90

Annex 2. Selected mortality data

Selected mortality data (2011): standardized death rate per 100 000 population and percentage changes from 2000. Non-negative percentage changes are outlined.

Cause of death	Sex	Greece		WHO European Region		EU15	
		Rate	Change	Rate	Change	Rate	Change
All causes	Both	547.9	-22.3%	788.3	-18.2%	523	-20.3%
	M	658.7	-23%	1047.6	-18.8%	656.2	-22.7%
	F	449.7	-21.4%	598.6	-17.5%	414.9	-18.7%
Infectious and parasitic diseases	M	5.3	16.3%	19	-18.1%	10.8	-5.1%
	F	4.2	42.4%	8.2	6.5%	7.1	11.3%
Malignant neoplasms	M	197.7	-11.2%	218.1	-12.9%	207	-15.6%
	F	105.3	-8.1%	123.7	-8.3%	125.2	-9.4%
Diseases of the circulatory system	M	246.7	-35%	472.5	-21.5%	196.3	-36.2%
	F	195.4	-34.7%	295.7	-23.7%	129.6	-34.3%
Diseases of the respiratory system	M	54.7	-16.3%	65.6	-31.5%	56	-30.3%
	F	39.9	-2.9%	29.2	-27.6%	31.2	-24.1%
Diseases of the digestive system	M	19.5	-14.5%	51.5	-1.5%	32	-19.4%
	F	10	-23.8%	27.4	0.5%	19.1	-17.8%
Symptoms, signs and ill-defined conditions	M	50.5	-2.9%	44.1	6%	22.5	1.7%
	F	47.7	21%	25.3	-1.8%	12.4	2.1%
External causes of injury and poisoning	M	41.9	-26.6%	99.2	-30.9%	44.1	-22.7%
	F	10.9	-36%	27.4	-28.7%	17.6	-21%
Motor vehicle road traffic injuries	M	17.1	-40%	14.6	-23.9%	7.9	-49.2%
	F	4.2	-45.8%	4.3	-26%	2.2	-54.8%
Suicide and self-inflicted injury	M	6.2	21.7%	21.6	-31.3%	14.2	-12.6%
	F	1.3	-2.2%	4.7	-27.1%	4.3	-14.3%
Homicide and intentional injury	M	2.5	69.4%	5.7	-53.3%	0.9	-31.5%
	F	0.5	-21.7%	1.7	-54.1%	0.4	-37.9%